Bop to the Jazz

By Carmel Reilly

"We will see some jazz!"
said Sall.

"Max Fox has a gig
at The Hut," said Bazz.

Sall pops on her red dress.

"I like that dress!" said Bazz.

"But look at **this** mess!"
said Sall.

"I will cut the frizz off," said Bazz.
"I can do it in a jiff."

"Yes! This frizz is bad," said Sall.

"I can fix it," said Bazz.

Cut, cut!

"I will cut this bit, too," said Bazz.

Cut, cut!

"Bazz!" yells Sall.

"I will buzz off the fuzz!"
said Bazz.

Buzz, buzz!

I can bop to the jazz
and I will not get frizz!

CHECKING FOR MEANING

1. What did Sall wear to The Hut? *(Literal)*

2. What did Bazz offer to do for Sall? *(Literal)*

3. How did Sall feel after her haircut? *(Inferential)*

EXTENDING VOCABULARY

jazz	*Jazz* is a style of music. What are the names of other styles of music you know? E.g. rock, classical, pop, country.
frizz	Look at the word *frizz*. What does this word mean? How many sounds can you hear in this word?
jiff	What is the meaning of *jiff* in this book? Is a jiff a long time or a short time?

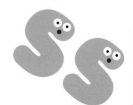

MOVING BEYOND THE TEXT

1. What instruments are played in jazz music?

2. Do you have long or short hair? Why?

3. Where do you go so you can dance to music?

4. Why do people like to sing and dance?

SPEED SOUNDS

| ff | ll | ss | zz |

PRACTICE WORDS

jazz

Sall

Bazz

mess

dress

will

fuzz

off

yells

frizz

jiff

Buzz

buzz